To: _____

From: _____

Published by Sourcebooks Casablanca, an imprint of Sourcebooks, Inc.
P.O. Box 4410, Naperville, Illinois 60567-4410
(630) 961-3900
Fax: (630) 961-2168
www.sourcebooks.com

ISBN-13: 978-1-4022-1092-1
ISBN-10: 1-4022-1092-2

Printed and bound in the United States of America
SP 10 9 8 7 6 5 4 3 2 1

COUPONS
for the
Bride

COUPONS
for the
Bride

I'm exhausted from trying on wedding gowns! I'm redeeming this coupon for a **trip to the lingerie store.** You pick the lingerie, and I'll **model it for you!**

COUPONS

for the

Bride

Honey, I've been working so hard on the wedding plans—I want to *relax,* and what better way than to get **one of your famous massages!**

COUPONS

for the

Bride

When I present this coupon, you will bring me **breakfast in bed.** There's no rush— we can sleep in **as late you want!**

COUPONS

for the

Bride

We've compromised on our *favorite music* for the reception. What would make me really happy is a mix CD from you of all my favorites. *I'll dance with you* to any song on it you want!

Let's take a break from looking at reception halls and **go to the movies!**

COUPONS

for the

Bride

Planning a wedding is so time-consuming! It seems like we never have any time alone together. **Come with me** to a quiet, remote place for a **romantic picnic.**

COUPONS

for the

Bride

When I present this coupon, you will bring me a **bouquet of my favorite flowers!**

COUPONS
for the
Bride

Let's take a break from trying to find the perfect ice sculpture for the reception: how about **taking a spin** around the ice with me? I'm redeeming this coupon for an **afternoon of ice skating.** If I lose my balance, I'll be so glad your arm's there to steady me!

COUPONS

for the

Bride

Forget the invitation designs for now!
Instead, *let's go to the park* and take
a *romantic stroll together.*

COUPONS

for the

Bride

I want to take you out for a karaoke night—you choose the song, and *I'll sing along.* We may not be on key, but *we're always in perfect harmony!*

I've been pretty stressed-out lately, so let's **take a deep breath**—and a glass of my **favorite wine!** You bring the bottle and I'll light some candles and **slip into something** a bit more comfortable!

COUPONS
for the
Bride

When I present this coupon, you get to take me on a **scenic drive** for an afternoon, *just the two of us.*

COUPONS

for the

Bride

Let's **take a break** from memorizing our lines for the big day and go to the *live* show of your choice.

COUPONS

for the

Bride

This coupon is good for one **private slow dance** to the song of my choice. No audience, no fancy clothes—**just the two of us** and some candlelight!

COUPONS

for the

Bride

I love hearing how much **you love me,** so I'm redeeming this coupon for a **heartfelt love note** from my beloved **husband-to-be!**

COUPONS

for the

Bride

Let's **relive our first date**—if it weren't for that night, we wouldn't be here today planning the rest of **our lives together!**

Coordinating hair, makeup, and manicure appointments for the big day isn't easy! What I really need, though, is a *soothing foot rub* from *you!*

COUPONS

for the

Bride

I'm all partied out! Let's have a **private party** of our own to *celebrate our love.* If you bring the *wine,* I'll bring the cheese and crackers!

COUPONS

for the

Bride

Let's take a break from contracts, schedules, and lists, and do **some romantic reading!** When I present this coupon, we'll spend the evening reading one another *romantic stories, poetry*—or perhaps something *erotic!*

COUPONS

for the

Bride

What's wedding cake without a little ice cream? I'm redeeming this coupon for a pint of my **favorite ice cream.** No cherry on top necessary—**just two spoons!**

COUPONS for the Bride

After a long day at work and running wedding errands, I'm too tired to cook dinner. I'm redeeming this coupon for some of my *favorite take-out*—with my *favorite person in the world!*

COUPONS

for the

Bride

Here's a stress reducing idea for the last week before the wedding: email me a *romantic quote or passage* daily for the entire week to remind me how happy I am that I'm about to *become your wife!*